Treating Your OCD with Exposure and Response (Ritual) Prevention Therapy

Treating Your OCD with Exposure and Response (Ritual) Prevention Therapy

Workbook

Second Edition

Elna Yadin • Edna B. Foa • Tracey K. Lichner

OXFORD
UNIVERSITY PRESS

Oxford University Press, Inc., publishes works that further
Oxford University's objective of excellence
in research, scholarship, and education.

Oxford New York
Auckland   Cape   Town   Dar es Salaam   Hong Kong   Karachi
Kuala Lumpur   Madrid   Melbourne   Mexico City   Nairobi
New Delhi   Shanghai   Taipei   Toronto

With offices in
Argentina   Austria   Brazil   Chile   Czech Republic   France   Greece
Guatemala   Hungary   Italy   Japan   Poland   Portugal   Singapore
South Korea   Switzerland   Thailand   Turkey   Ukraine   Vietnam

Published by Oxford University Press, Inc.
198 Madison Avenue, New York, New York 10016

www.oup.com

Oxford is a registered trademark of Oxford University Press

ISBN-13 9780195335293 Paper

14

Printed in Canada
on acid-free paper

About Treatments *ThatWork*™

One of the most difficult problems confronting patients with various disorders and diseases is finding the best help available. Everyone is aware of friends or family who have sought treatment from a seemingly reputable practitioner, only to find out later from another doctor that the original diagnosis was wrong or the treatments recommended were inappropriate or perhaps even harmful. Most patients, or family members, address this problem by reading everything they can about their symptoms, seeking out information on the Internet, or aggressively "asking around" to tap knowledge from friends and acquaintances. Governments and healthcare policymakers are also aware that people in need don't always get the best treatments—something they refer to as "variability in healthcare practices."

Now healthcare systems around the world are attempting to correct this variability by introducing "evidence-based practice." This simply means that it is in everyone's interest that patients get the most up-to-date and effective care for a particular problem. Healthcare policymakers have also recognized that it is very useful to give consumers of healthcare as much information as possible, so that they can make intelligent decisions in a collaborative effort to improve health and mental health. This series, Treatments *That Work*™, is designed to accomplish just that. Only the latest and most effective interventions for particular problems are described, in user-friendly language. To be included in this series, each treatment program must pass the highest standards of evidence available, as determined by a scientific advisory board. Thus, when individuals suffering from these problems or their family members seek out an expert clinician who is familiar with these interventions and decides that they are appropriate, they will have confidence that they are receiving the best care available. Of course, only your healthcare professional can decide on the right mix of treatments for you.

This workbook is written for people with obsessive-compulsive disorder (OCD) who are interested in learning how to control their obsessional thoughts and compulsive rituals using a treatment called Exposure and Ritual Prevention (EX/RP).

You may have been invited to read this book by your clinician who plans to teach you EX/RP, which has been proven effective in reducing OCD symptoms in numerous scientific studies. Or you might be reading this book because you are curious about how you might use EX/RP to learn how to better manage your symptoms.

This EX/RP treatment program is broken down into 17 to 20 biweekly treatment sessions, during which you will be exposed to situations and places that trigger your OCD symptoms. These "exposures" are designed to be gradual so that over time you come to realize that the things you fear will not necessarily occur if you do not perform your rituals. Some exposures will be supervised by your therapist, but you will also be asked to practice on your own at home.

Although some individuals do not respond as well as we would hope, EX/RP is the single most effective treatment for OCD available, and offers you the best chance for recovery. If you are motivated to engage in treatment, there is a very good chance you will experience a decrease in your symptoms and potential mastery over your OCD.

David H. Barlow, Editor-in-Chief,
Treatments *That Work*™
Boston, MA

Acknowledgments

I want to acknowledge the contribution of Dr. Michael Kozak to my conceptualization of the psychopathology that underlies OCD and the mechanisms that underlie exposure and ritual prevention, which are explicated in the manual. Indeed, the present manual is an update and expansion of a previous manual, "Mastery of Your Obsessions and Compulsions," coauthored by Dr. Kozak and myself. I also want to thank Drs. Michael Leibowitz and Blair Simpson for the insight they provided into my view of OCD through many years of collaborations. My thanks are extended to my collaborators at the Center for the Treatment and Study of Anxiety over the past 30 years. Lastly, I want to thank the patients who taught me so much about how to help them.

-Edna B. Foa

To my dear family and friends who taught me about loyalty and generosity; to my colleagues, past and present, whose work is incorporated in this book; and last, but not least, to our patients, together with whom we have learned about struggle, compassion, and triumph.

-Elna Yadin

To my wonderful, vibrant sisters—you keep alive the determined spirit of our parents, and your love, encouragement, and friendship mean the world to me.

-Tracey K. Lichner

Contents

Chapter 1   *Introduction*

Goals

▣ Understand the nature of obsessive-compulsive disorder (OCD)

▣ Learn how OCD is treated

OCD: Some Facts

OCD is a neuropsychological disorder that includes two characteristics: (1) Obsessions, which are recurrent and persistent thoughts, impulses, or images that are experienced as intrusive and inappropriate and cause marked anxiety or distress, and (2) Compulsions (or rituals), which are repetitive behaviors, thoughts, or images that the person feels compelled to perform in response to an obsession or a certain rule that must be applied rigidly. Most of the time there is a relationship between the compulsion and the obsession in that the compulsion is performed to neutralize or reduce the distress that accompanies the obsession.

As you probably know, the symptoms of OCD may include unwanted or upsetting doubts, or other thoughts about harm, contamination, sex, religious themes, health, or other such topics. Rituals may include excessive washing, checking and re-checking, praying in a specific rigid way, repeating routine activities or actions, or special thoughts designed to counteract negative thoughts. You are probably also aware of certain situations, places, or objects (that you may usually avoid or want to avoid) that trigger your obsessions and urges to ritualize.

Experts estimate that several million people in the United States suffer from OCD. The onset of OCD typically occurs between early adolescence and young adulthood, although in some people OCD begins as young as 2 years old or as late as age 60. Males generally develop the disorder earlier, in their teenage years, while females develop the disorder in young adulthood. Among adults, the incidence of OCD is equal for men and women. In most cases, OCD symptoms develop gradually, although in a small number of people they start suddenly. Without treatment, the course of OCD is chronic and can fluctuate in severity. Although effective treatment significantly improves quality of life among individuals with OCD, many persons with OCD suffer for years before seeking treatment.

How Is OCD Treated?

In the past four decades, scientific knowledge about the specific symptoms and potential causes of OCD has greatly increased, and this knowledge has led to more effective treatment strategies for sufferers. The psychological treatment program that has received the most scientific evidence is called Exposure and Response (or Ritual) Prevention (EX/RP or ERP). The EX/RP treatment program includes the following components.

Introductory Phase

- An explanation of the cognitive-behavioral model of OCD

- A description of the treatment program

- Collecting information about the specific clinical features of your OCD, including inquiring about the history of your OCD, exploring the onset and course of your OCD symptoms, identifying triggers that elicit your obsessions, as well as outlining your compulsions (rituals) and avoidance patterns

- Teaching you how to monitor your obsessions and compulsions on a daily basis

Treatment Phase

- Collaboratively creating a hierarchy of situations and activities that trigger your distress and rating them on a subjective distress or discomfort scale

- Designing *in vivo* ("real life") exposures to help you confront cues, including objects, words, images, or situations that make you anxious or distressed; you now do compulsions in reaction to these or you try to avoid them altogether

- Designing imaginal exposures to help you confront in imagination the details of the negative consequences you expect if you do not avoid or ritualize after confronting situations that trigger your obsessional distress

- Teaching you ritual prevention, which means helping you refrain from doing the behavioral or mental acts that you do now to reduce your obsessional distress or prevent the negative consequences from happening

- Discussing what happened to your obsessional anxiety/distress during exposure and ritual prevention and re-evaluating the merit of the beliefs about the predicted feared consequences

- Discussing strategies to maintain the gains made in treatment and prevent relapsing in the future

The *in vivo* and imaginal exposures, together with overcoming your avoidance and ritual prevention, are the core of the EX/RP treatment. Studies show that these components are essential for a successful outcome. Numerous studies have demonstrated that the majority of people who comply with EX/RP treatment have benefited from this program, and there is hope that you will too. This workbook will help guide you step by step as you go through the program.

Risks and Benefits of this Treatment Program

Benefits

Almost four decades of research has supported the effectiveness of EX/RP in reducing OCD symptoms and providing long-term management of the symptoms. By reducing the time, energy, and resources spent on OCD, sufferers are able to improve the quality of their lives and are able to pursue their goals and maintain their relationships.

Risks

The primary risks associated with EX/RP are discomfort and emotional distress when confronting anxiety-provoking objects, situations, thoughts, and images in the initial stages of the treatment. EX/RP is designed to help you confront the situations and objects that evoke obsessional distress, which will temporarily increase in order for you to learn that the anxiety or distress will indeed go down on its own, without having to do rituals or to avoid the triggers. This can be very uncomfortable at first. That is why this program recommends doing it with the help of a trained therapist who will help you tolerate the anxiety/distress and work your way through it. Once you are able to tolerate the distress without ritualizing or avoiding, you will begin feeling a lot better. The benefit of the treatment is that you will no longer have to engage in the tedious and time-consuming compulsions and will feel both relief and freedom from "slavery" to the OCD.

The Role of Medications

Parallel to the development of effective cognitive-behavioral therapy for OCD, there was a development of medication treatment for the disorder. The first medication to be approved for treatment of adult OCD was clomipramine (Anafranil®), and since then many of the selective serotonin reuptake inhibitors (SSRIs) were added. These include fluvoxamine (Luvox®), fluoxetine (Prozac®), sertraline (Zoloft®), and paroxetine (Paxil®). Recently, controlled studies have shown an improved effect of SSRI treatment by augmenting it with atypical antipsychotic medications such as risperidone (Risperdal®), olanzapine (Zyprexa®), and quetiapine (Seroquel®). Augmentation with these medications may be considered in patients who have substantial residual symptoms with the standard medications and who will not accept, or do not have access to, EX/RP.

If you are already taking this type of medication and still suffer from OCD, you can stay on your medication and go through the EX/RP program because there is no evidence that these medications interfere with this treatment.

Outline of this Program

The treatment program consists of approximately 17 sessions that are generally 90 to 120 minutes each. The sessions can be conducted either once weekly, twice weekly, or daily. The daily program is called "intensive" treatment. This workbook is divided into chapters that describe what will happen in each session. Each chapter includes the techniques you will use and instructions on how to use them, practice exercises, and all the necessary handouts and forms that you will need to help you maximize your success.

Structure of Sessions

Session 1 begins with the therapist collecting information about your general history, your OCD symptoms, the history of your OCD, and previous treatment you received. In Session 1 the therapist will give you an explanation of OCD, will present the rationale for and description of the treatment, and will introduce you to the practice of daily self-monitoring of obsessions and compulsions.

Session 2 begins with a review of self-monitoring sheets and continues with gathering of information that will help generate a plan for your treatment. Next, using the scale of Subjective Units of Discomfort or Distress (SUDS), the therapist and you collaboratively create a list of situations and objects that you will gradually confront during treatment.

Session 3 begins with a review of self-monitoring sheets, and introduces the exposure and ritual prevention treatment components. Your therapist and you will choose *in vivo* exposures and ritual prevention to practice in session, and you will practice those exposures and ritual prevention at home. Your therapist will also show you how to monitor your SUDS during the exposures, so you will be writing them down. This will help you see for yourself how your anxiety or distress diminishes even without ritualizing or avoiding. It will also help you realize that the negative consequences of exposure and ritual prevention that you anticipate do not actually happen.

Session 4 begins with a homework review and introduces the imaginal exposure component (as needed). Your therapist will teach you how to create an imaginal exposure script that will address your feared consequences and worst-case scenarios that cannot be done in real life. Next, you and your therapist will choose situations from your *in vivo* list to practice in session, you will practice those items at home, and you will monitor your anxiety.

Intermediate sessions will follow a similar format, choosing increasingly more challenging situations or objects that you are avoiding for exposures at each visit, At approximately the eighth session, you will be ready to confront the most distressing item on your list. During the 9th through 16th sessions you will repeat previous exposures and add new ones that were not included in your original list but that, through monitoring, you have discovered bother you and cause you distress. If practical and necessary, your therapist will visit your home once or twice to coach you with exposures and help you implement EX/RP at home The therapist will make additional visits to your home if you continue to have difficulty with home-based practices.

In the final sessions your therapist will evaluate your progress and help prepare you for returning to regular behavior. This will include discussion of strategies that can maximize the maintenance of your gains and prevent you from relapsing to your old OCD habits. While your therapist will incorporate discussion about how to prevent relapse throughout the treatment, in the final session the therapist will place a special emphasis on that aspect. The final part of the final session is devoted to discussing follow-up phone calls or visits, and saying goodbye.

Chapter 2　　　　*Is This Program Right For You?*

Goals

- Determine if this program is right for you
- Enhance your motivation for treatment

Who Can Benefit From Exposure and Response (Ritual) Prevention?

If you are having obsessions and compulsions that are causing you anxiety and distress and interfere with your ability to navigate through everyday activities because they consume a lot of time and energy, you are a good candidate for EX/RP. Sometimes OCD sufferers also have additional psychiatric problems. However, if your OCD is your primary problem, if it is what bothers you the most, you are a good candidate for EX/RP. If, however, you are battling extremely severe depression that would make it difficult for you to muster the energy and mental resources needed to apply EX/RP in full, or if you are feeling actively suicidal, then we would suggest that you first receive treatment for the depression, and when you are feeling less depressed you can then engage in EX/RP for your OCD.

We do not recommend treatment with EX/RP if you currently have strong urges and a plan to commit suicide or to harm other people or you have attempted these behaviors in the past few months. If you are suffering from suicidal or homicidal behaviors and strong thoughts, we recommend you seek treatment for those first before engaging in EX/RP.

Enhancing Motivation for Treatment

It is difficult for people who suffer from OCD to confront the situations that trigger their obsessional anxiety or distress without performing compulsions to reduce that distress. You must have heard numerous times during your life people saying: "It doesn't make sense to worry about those things" or "Just don't do the compulsions!" Those who have never experienced OCD cannot imagine why someone would choose to do repeated compulsions or avoid situations that trigger discomfort altogether. Therapists with expertise in treating OCD patients know that you don't *choose* to ritualize; instead, you feel *compelled* to do them because the distress is so painful. Your therapist is your ally in the treatment and he or she will discuss with you motivational issues in order to support you in your journey to overcome OCD:

1. Treatment is framed as a team effort spearheaded by you, with the help of your therapist (and other members of your support system), to wage a battle against your OCD.

2. Consider all the things that you want to accomplish but are unable to now because of your OCD. How would your life be better if your OCD were in remission or at least in the margins of your everyday existence? Think about things such as returning to work or getting a better job; establishing relationships or having more time for existing relationships; engaging in enjoyable activities such as reading books, traveling, devoting time to a hobby; or being able to do things with greater ease, such as practicing religion, doing homework, accomplishing tasks at work, etc.

3. Doing exposures is more beneficial for you than just talking about doing exposures, so find the courage to practice EX/RP as soon as possible and as often as possible ("The more you do it, the easier it gets").

4. Make sure not to "draw a line in the sand," such as deciding *a priori* that you will *never ever* confront a certain situation without performing the compulsions that will reduce your obsessional distress. Remember that EX/RP is based on gradually going up a hierarchy of difficulty, and things that look impossible early on will become easier when the time comes to approach them. It is like looking at the peak of a high mountain from the base, thinking "there is no way I can get there

from here!" As you begin to climb, the goal of reaching the peak becomes more attainable.

5. It is important not to leave any stones unturned. OCD sufferers sometime minimize the situation by saying that a symptom is not that bad and that the rituals don't take that much time and effort, so it's not worth the bother to tackle them. It is important to remember that what maintains the endless ritualizing is the rituals' ability to decrease your obsessional distress, even if the relief is short-lived. This means that the habit of reducing the anxiety or distress through compulsions maintains and even strengthens the OCD. Therefore, no matter how trivial the compulsion is, it needs to be eliminated. Continuing to ritualize even a little is like a surgeon leaving "just a few" cancerous cells when removing a tumor.

6. Your therapist will be delighted to share with you examples from other OCD patients he or she had treated who have benefited greatly from EX/RP, as well as ones who have not applied the treatment as intended and have experienced less success or have relapsed. We can all learn from the collective experience with this treatment and through the generosity of patients who have done EX/RP.

Chapter 3   *Session 1*

Goals

- Information gathering

- Learn about OCD

- Learn about the rationale for treatment

- Understand the treatment program

- Introduce self-monitoring

Information Gathering

The first session will begin by providing your therapist with information about the following: your age, marital/relationship status, children, living arrangement, and current work situation. Also, your therapist will ask you about your general history, such as your medical history, education, employment, financial situation, relationships with family, relationships with friends, dating history, and marital history. After obtaining you general history, your therapist will collect detailed information about your obsessive-compulsive symptoms. A thorough understanding of your symptoms will allow your therapist to tailor the therapy procedures specifically for you.

What is OCD?

OCD is a set of symptoms that, as you know, are called obsessive-compulsive symptoms. These include thoughts, feelings, and behaviors that are extremely unpleasant, unproductive, and difficult to get rid of on your own. Usually, these involve thoughts, images, or impulses that come to mind against your will. These thoughts are accompanied by unwanted feelings of extreme distress/anxiety (also guilt, shame, or disgust) and strong urges to do something to reduce the distress. One way in which people try to reduce their anxiety is by avoiding situations, objects, and thoughts that evoke this anxiety. However, with people who suffer from OCD, avoidance or escape from the things that evoke their anxiety does not work well and they develop a habit of doing things that help reduce their distress, even if for a short time.

As is the case with all people with OCD, your attempts to avoid the situations or thoughts that cause you the distress do not work well and, therefore, you developed habits of doing certain actions or thinking special thoughts to try to reduce your distress. We call these *habits*, *rituals*, or *compulsions*. Unfortunately, performing these rituals also does not work all that well, and the distress decreases for only a short time before coming back again. Often, you find yourself doing more and more rituals to reduce your distress, but even then, the rituals reduce the distress only temporarily. Eventually you are putting so much time and energy into the rituals, which do not work well anyway, that other areas of your life get seriously disrupted.

Why Choose EX/RP Treatment?

You may wonder how is it helpful to expose yourself to places, objects, situations, or thoughts that you have attempted to avoid at a great cost, and that will actually make you uncomfortable. We know that when people are exposed to situations that provoke their obsessions, they *do* become anxious or distressed. This is a common reaction for people with OCD. As we mentioned above, we also know that avoiding the triggers for obsessions or ritualizing in response to them does not work well in the long run and has not worked well for you, either. This is why your therapist will spend some time discussing with you how the exposure and ritual prevention treatment (EX/RP) will help you overcome your OCD symptoms, and your therapist will teach you how to implement it in a way that is most likely to help you maintain your treatment gains. You will learn about exposures in real life (called *in vivo* exposures) and exposures in imagination (called imaginal exposures).

How Does *In Vivo* Exposure Work?

When you confront a situation that causes you distress and you stay in the situation for a long enough time without escaping or doing rituals, you will learn several things. First, you will learn that the anxiety/distress does not last forever. In fact, it decreases even without escaping, avoiding, or ritualizing. Also, you will find out that at the same time that your anxiety decreases, your urge to ritualize and to escape from the situation also decreases. This way, your habit of performing rituals will weaken.

If your fears include disastrous consequences such as dying from illness, or causing a fire or a flood, you will learn that by confronting the situations that cause you distress without escaping them or performing rituals, you will realize that the things you are afraid will happen if you don't ritualize actually do not happen. You will also learn that anxiety does not last forever and that you will not have a "nervous breakdown." On the contrary, after you do the same exposure several times, you will feel that **you** are in control and that you can overcome your OCD.

If your feared consequences are about bad things happening in the remote future or things that are vague or not easily subject to disproving, by confronting the triggers you will learn to live with doubt and to tolerate the uncertainty just like most people, who don't really know what the future holds. Avoiding, escaping, or ritualizing in response to the triggers only gives you the illusion of control over bad events that can occur in the future, while in fact these actions strengthen your OCD symptoms in the present.

If you cannot do exposure in real life to your fears because they are dangerous, illegal, immoral, or impossible to create, we will use imaginal exposure. To help you with these objects, images, situations, or thoughts that trigger these disastrous consequences, obviously we do not recommend *in vivo* exposures. Instead, your therapist will teach you how to do exposures in imagination to the worst-case scenario that your OCD is presenting to you, coupled with ritual prevention, so you can learn that although allowing the thoughts in increases your distress level, you can tolerate that, and your anxiety will decrease, just like with the *in vivo* exposures.

How Does Imaginal Exposure Work?

Your therapist will explain to you how imaginal exposure works to reduce your OCD symptoms. Imaginal exposure can help you in several ways. In imaginal exposure you and your therapist will write down in detail the things that you are afraid will happen to you or to other people because you did not avoid them or because you did not ritualize enough. Your therapist will ask you to repeatedly imagine that these things actually happen. How will imagining that these bad things actually happen help you?

First, you will learn that repeatedly imagining that the terrible things you are afraid of will indeed happen will help you get used to these thoughts. You will gradually be able to think about them without experiencing high levels of anxiety or distress.

Second, you will learn that even though your anxiety decreases when thinking about the things you are afraid of happening, you are not likely to start engaging in those fear-evoking behaviors. For example, getting used to intrusive bad thoughts about contracting a terminal disease in the future will not turn you into a careless person who is oblivious to healthy lifestyle practices.

Third, just like with the *in vivo* exposure, you will learn to accept your negative thoughts and feelings and be able to cope with them rather than to try and get rid of them. This will teach you that you can experience distress without "falling apart," and that you can establish a sense of mastery in the face of the negative emotions.

Another reason why imaginal exposure works is that it will teach you that thinking about the horrible thoughts or images does not make them come true. Thinking about something does not make it happen.

When you learn all these things, you will realize that you do not need to work hard to push your unwanted thoughts out of your mind or to perform rituals to prevent the bad things from happening.

In summary, this treatment will help you realize that your OCD beliefs are mistaken, and through experience doing exposures with ritual prevention you will learn to correct them.

During the next session or two, your therapist will continue to collect information about your symptoms to identify the situations and thoughts that generate your discomfort or anxiety. Together, you will then arrange these situations in a hierarchy according to the degree of distress they generate. Exposure treatment will begin in Session 3. Exposure involves confronting situations and thoughts that you avoid because they generate anxiety and urges to carry out ritualistic behavior. You will meet with your therapist to conduct exposure practices under supervision. You will learn how to do exposures so that on the days when you do not meet, you can practice successfully on your own. You will have a scheduled telephone contact once a week on one of the days you do not meet with your therapist face to face. The purpose of the phone call is to check in, to assess your progress, and to receive encouragement and support.

Self-Monitoring

It is very important for the success of your treatment that you and your therapist have an accurate picture of how much you engage in obsessive thinking and compulsive behavior. Having a clear picture of how much of your time is taken up by your OCD will help you and your therapist to monitor your progress and to adjust the treatment program accordingly. Therefore, you will be asked to record symptoms every day during this week.

Since it is not always easy to report accurately on how much you engage in obsessive-compulsive behavior, you and your therapist will spend some time now and in the next session going over some rules for how to record symptoms, using the Self-Monitoring Form in this workbook. Use the following general rules to guide your monitoring:

- Make sure to record both overt and mental rituals.

- Keep track of the time you spend on your rituals.

- It is best not to save the recording to the end of the day or the beginning of the next day, because you will likely forget details.

■ Write a short sentence to describe the trigger for ritualizing.

■ Use a descriptive word or two and not a long paragraph for each ritual.

Homework

✎ Complete Self-Monitoring Forms each day and bring them to the next session.

✎ Review the "Obsessive-Compulsive Disorder: Some Facts" section of the workbook to solidify your understanding of the disorder.

✎ Make sure you are available and prepared for the inter-session phone call.

Chapter 4

Session 2

Goals

- Review self-monitoring
- Review the model of OCD and discuss the rationale for treatment
- Create hierarchy of exposures

Self-Monitoring Review

The session will begin by going over the Self-Monitoring Forms you have completed. Your therapist will help you elaborate on these as needed.

Model of OCD and Rationale for Treatment

Your therapist will review with you the OCD model and will go over the rationale for the EX/RP treatment to make sure it makes sense to you. Understanding your OCD and the rationale for the treatment will increase the chances that you will greatly benefit from the treatment. Throughout the session you and your therapist will continue to examine your specific OCD symptoms to begin to develop a treatment plan tailored to your symptoms.

Create a Hierarchy of Exposures

As you know, the treatment program consists of gradually approaching situations that provoke your obsessional distress. To prepare your treatment program, you and your therapist will generate a list of the specific situations that provoke your OCD anxiety and distress and then rate each situation according to how much discomfort it generates in you when you confront it. To communicate to your therapist your degree of distress in each situation, you will learn how to describe your level of distress in numbers using the Subjective Units of Distress (or Discomfort) Scale (SUDS for short). This scale ranges from 0 to 100, where 0 means that you feel no discomfort whatsoever and 100 indicate that you are extremely distressed, the most anxious/distress you've ever felt. Your therapist will ask you to describe a situation that caused you no distress at all; that will be your 0 point. You will then describe a situation you experienced that caused you the worst distress ever; that will be your 100 point. Next, you will identify a situation during which you were distressed but still found it manageable; that will be your 50 point.

After establishing the SUDS anchors, you and your therapist will arrange the situations you identified from the least distressing to the most distressing, which is called a hierarchy. To help you better understand this task, see the following examples of hierarchies. Note that these case descriptions are for illustration purposes only and are therefore somewhat general. Your hierarchy will include many more situations tailored very specifically to your individual set of triggers.

Case Example: Amy

Amy felt contaminated by bodily fluids, including blood, feces, urine, and sweat and by contact with others. Her feared consequence was contracting a debilitating disease. Each treatment session included exposure to contaminants.

The following hierarchy was constructed for Amy. Note that these items all have in common her feared consequences of contracting a disease.

1. Touching doorknobs (50 SUDS)

2. Handling newspapers used by others (60 SUDS)

3. Touching sweaty surfaces (75 SUDS)

4. Going to the bathroom without washing (80 SUDS)

5. Using public bathrooms (90 SUDS)

6. Shaking hands with Red Cross workers (100 SUDS)

Case Example: Mike

Mike feared harming others when driving his car or as a result of failing to check appliances, locks, lights, and such at home. He worried about his 4-year-old daughter, fearing that he would drop her while carrying her over a hard floor or that she would fall downstairs because he was not supervising her enough. To prevent these catastrophes, Mike checked repeatedly.

The following hierarchy was constructed for Mike:

1. Turning lights and stove on or off without looking back (50 SUDS)

2. Locking doors and windows without checking (60 SUDS)

3. Leaving electrical appliances plugged in (70 SUDS)

4. Imaginal exposure about being responsible for his daughter falling down the basement stairs because of lack of supervision (75 SUDS)

5. Carrying daughter while walking on hard-surfaced floors (85 SUDS)

6. Driving on highway without retracing route (100 SUDS)

Case Example: Ryan

Ryan feared "turning into someone else," which to him meant that by coming in contact with someone he perceived as "bad," he would acquire those undesirable characteristics and lose his own "essence." Ryan avoided places in his local area (such as school, swimming pool, library) where he used to encounter the "contaminating" individual, and engaged in an elaborate cleaning and decontaminating ritual before entering his own room.

The following hierarchy was constructed for Ryan:

1. Using the contaminating person's name (50 SUDS)

2. Going to the library (60 SUDS)

3. Going swimming at the local swimming pool (70 SUDS)

4. Bringing book bag and swimming trunks into the house (80 SUDS)

5. Sitting on the bed in own room without decontaminating (90 SUDS)

Homework

✎ Continue to fill out your Self-Monitoring Forms each day and bring them to the next session.

✎ Review the "Understanding Exposure and Ritual Prevention (EX/RP) Therapy for OCD" section of the workbook to solidify your understanding of EX/RP.

✎ Make sure you are available and prepared for the inter-session phone call.

Chapter 5   *Session 3*

Goals

- Review self-monitoring
- Conduct *in vivo* exposure
- Instructions for self-exposure

Self-Monitoring Review

The session will begin by the therapist going over the Self-Monitoring Forms you completed. Your therapist will help you identify when the triggers occurred and what exactly you had to do to alleviate the distress associated with them. Together you and your therapist will explore the nuances of your feared consequences, the things you are afraid will happen if you confront a situation that evokes your obsessional concern without ritualizing, and will identify your worst fear.

In Vivo Exposure

Your therapist and you will begin with the *in vivo* exposure that you both planned for that day's session. Your therapist will describe, at the beginning of the session, exactly what the exposure practice will be. During the *in vivo* exposures, you and your therapist may discuss the changes in your anxiety levels and thoughts about your feared consequences, so you can realize that your feared consequences do not necessarily occur.

After exposure practice with your therapist's supervision, you will be given instructions for self-exposure. It is crucial that you are able to do exposures on your own. Therefore, for homework, the therapist will ask you to do an exposure that is as similar as possible to the situation you practiced in session with your therapist. Generally, the homework exposures should last for about 2 hours each day. If you can't continually do exposures for 2-hour periods because of special circumstances, you and your therapist will devise an exposure plan that will allow you to experience a reduction in your anxiety level.

Sometimes your therapist may ask you to do a new exposure as homework if it cannot be done in the office because of the logistics of the situation. For example, you may need to touch objects at home or elsewhere that can't be brought into the office or easily reached from the office.

You and your therapist will agree on several items from the hierarchy that you will practice before the next session. Record the assignment on the Exposure Homework Recording Form in the workbook. Do the exposure at home just as you did in the session. That means you will do the exposures without rituals for a long enough time for your anxiety or distress to decrease. A useful guideline is to do each exposure for 1 full hour, or until you notice that your distress has decreased by approximately 50%. It will not be helpful for you to confront the situation and then to leave it before you notice feeling a little better. Every 10 minutes during the exposure, write down your anxiety level on the Exposure Homework Recording Form.

Be ready to discuss the homework exposures at the next phone contact with your therapist. If you have any problems or comments about the homework, you can write a brief note on the Exposure Homework Recording Form as a reminder to raise them during the phone contact.

✎ Continue to fill out your Self-Monitoring Forms each day and bring them to the next session.

✎ Read the "Patient Rules for Ritual Prevention" section of the workbook.

✎ Practice the *in vivo* exposures assigned during the session, writing down your SUDS and comments on the Exposure Homework Recording Form.

✎ Make sure you are available and prepared for the inter-session phone call.

Chapter 6

Session 4

Goals

- Review self-monitoring and exposure homework
- Introduce and conduct imaginal exposure
- Conduct *in vivo* exposure
- Instructions for self-exposure

Self-Monitoring and Exposure Homework Review

As usual, the session will begin by going over the Self-Monitoring Forms you completed. You and your therapist will go over the *in vivo* exposure homework and discuss your experience with it. This will include discussion of the changes you noticed in your anxiety or distress levels as you were doing the exposures repeatedly, and what you have learned about your ability to tolerate the discomfort.

Imaginal Exposure

Some situations cannot be practiced in an *in vivo* setting because they are dangerous or illegal. In those cases, your therapist will introduce you to a powerful technique in the treatment of OCD called imaginal exposure. Imaginal exposure can be used for those suffering from the following types of obsessions: accidentally harming others, such as running someone over with your car; having unwanted blasphemous thoughts, like a fear of going to hell; or experiencing unwanted sexual intrusions. In these situations, imaginal exposure employs a person's ability to use his or her imagination as a vehicle for exposures that cannot easily or ethically be done in real life.

1. It gives you the opportunity to deliberately "invite in" the obsessional thoughts and images that you typically try to avoid or that you do compulsions to "cross out." Since these are consequences that cannot be confronted in real life, you will be using your imagination to do so. These include feared consequences that are either in the future, vague, impractical, unethical, or illegal—for example, obsessions about contracting cancer, losing one's essence, causing someone's death, or committing a crime.

2. It teaches you that you are able to experience distress without "falling apart," and gives you a sense of mastery in the face of the negative emotions.

3. It allows you to imagine the entire progression of events leading to the ultimate feared consequences.

4. When repeated, it allows you to experience a gradual reduction in the anxiety or distress caused by your obsessions, just like watching a horror movie over and over again. The first time you watch the movie will create a great amount of fear. But as you watch the same movie repeatedly, the scary details will begin to become predictable and, therefore, less distressing. If you watched the movie 100 times, it would likely become boring!

5. It help you to realize that having horrendous thoughts or images does not necessarily make them come true. This gives you the opportunity to learn that you do not have the control to cause a bad consequence by thinking about it, nor do you have the control to prevent it by not thinking about it or by performing rituals.

6. It teaches you that the likelihood of such negative events is rather low and that the cost you are paying to protect yourself or others from these low-probability events is rather high. The cost to you often manifests in many forms, such as loss of time, energy, money, career, and relationships.

How Is Imaginal Exposure Done?

You and your therapist will come up with a script that clearly depicts the sequence of your obsessional fears, including the absolute worst-case scenario. Either you or your therapist will make an audio recording of the script. You will be asked to close your eyes so that you won't be distracted. You will try to picture the scene as fully and as vividly as possible, as if you are experiencing it in the moment. Every few minutes your therapist will ask you to rate your anxiety/distress level on the SUDS scale (from 0 to 100).

In Vivo Exposure and Ritual Prevention

You will engage in the *in vivo* exposures planned for this session in the same manner as described in the previous session.

Instructions for Self-Exposure

Similar to Session 3, after exposure practice with your therapist's supervision, you will practice the exposures on your own on the days when you don't have sessions. During this early stage of treatment, be sure to practice for homework those exposures that your therapist assigned to you during the session. If imaginal exposure was conducted and audio-taped during the session, your homework will include listening to the entire recording without interruption for about an hour, or until your anxiety decreases by approximately 50%. You should listen to the recording with your eyes closed at times you are not busy with anything else. You should record your SUDS level just before starting the recording and after it is over.

Homework

 ✎ Continue to fill out your Self-Monitoring Forms each day and bring them to the next session.

✎ Practice listening to your imaginal exposure, writing down your SUDS and comments on the Imaginal Exposure Homework Recording Form.

✎ Practice the *in vivo* exposures assigned during the session, writing down your SUDS and comments on the Exposure Homework Recording Form.

✎ Make sure you are available and prepared for the inter-session phone call.

Chapter 7 *Intermediate Sessions*

Goals

- Review self-monitoring and exposure homework

- Conduct *in vivo* and/or imaginal exposure

- Home visits (as needed)

- Review progress

- Address relapse prevention

The following sessions are conducted according to the format used for Sessions 3 and 4. Exposure and ritual prevention are practiced at each visit, with increasingly difficult exposures attempted through the sessions. At approximately Session 8, you will be ready to confront the highest item on your hierarchy. The work from Session 8 on involves repeating or varying previous exposures and introducing relevant situations that were not included in your original hierarchy. Self-monitoring and ritual prevention will be used throughout therapy. At the start of each session, you and your therapist will together examine your homework and self-monitoring forms. At the end of each session your therapist will assign you homework and establish with you a time for a phone check-in.

Home Visits (as needed)

For many OCD patients, the home environment can become an especially challenging place. If needed and practical, your therapist will do one or two home visits, with additional visits when applicable. These visits give your therapist the opportunity to observe your functioning in your home environment, to identify areas of difficulty, and to coach you in creating exposures in that environment. Home visits can be done at any point during the exposure sessions (i.e., from Session 3 on).

Progress Review

Periodically, your therapist will review with you the progress you have made. You will be discussing what differences you notice in your behavior, your tolerance for obsessional thoughts, and your ability to function in various environments (e.g., home, work, social situations). Your therapist will ask you whether you have any difficulty completing homework exposures and/or ritual prevention. You will have the opportunity to discuss any difficulties you may have and learn to problem-solve and overcome obstacles. The better you are able to do so, the more success you will experience in treatment.

Relapse Prevention

EX/RP teaches you to be your own therapist so that you can continue to apply the principles once treatment is over. Knowing how to handle future OCD challenges is the key to relapse prevention. Relapse prevention will be introduced early and revisited periodically. You should know that, due to the nature of the disorder, you are likely to have intrusive thoughts from time to time, even if you have improved significantly in treatment. Therefore, be mindful of the following:

- The experience of intrusive thoughts is not a sign of a relapse. After all, even people without OCD experience odd or unusual thoughts from time to time.

- The key to relapse prevention is your reaction to the intrusive thought. Although it is fine to recognize the thought ("Hmmm, that's an unusual thought!"), you should not respond to it by trying to make it go away or by neutralizing it (crossing it out with a compulsion).

- For your OCD symptoms to remain in remission, you must refrain from engaging in any rituals (whether behavioral or mental). You should also make sure not to avoid or stay away from situations that trigger your OCD symptoms.

Your therapist will help you learn how to set up your own exposures, since you might need to do this on your own in the future if a particular thought begins to cause you a problem. Your therapist will encourage you to take a progressively more active role in your treatment by suggesting and designing your own exposures and homework assignments. Also, you will eventually be encouraged to seize opportunities to work on your OCD symptoms as they naturally occur in the environment. This practice of "leaning into the anxiety" (rather than running away from it) is predictive of a good long-term outcome.

Homework

Continue to fill out your Self-Monitoring Forms each day and bring them to the next session.

Practice listening to your imaginal exposure, writing down your SUDS and comments on the Imaginal Exposure Homework Recording Form.

Practice the *in vivo* exposures assigned during the session, writing down your SUDS and comments on the Exposure Homework Recording Form.

Make sure you are available and prepared for the inter-session phone call.

Chapter 8   *Final Session*

Goals

- Review progress

- Prepare for return to "normal" behavior

- Address relapse prevention

- Schedule follow-up phone contacts

- Conclude therapy

The final session includes an evaluation of your progress in treatment and preparation for your return to regular behavior, with discussion of strategies to maximize relapse prevention. Although relapse prevention has been discussed throughout the treatment, a special emphasis will be placed on that aspect during the final session.

Progress Review

At the final session of exposure, your therapist will devote extra time to reviewing the progress you have made throughout treatment. Together, you will evaluate the success of what you have accomplished or what else is needed to improve your outcome. You will discuss the differences you notice in your own behavior, in your tolerance for obsessional thoughts, and in your ability to function in various situations. This is important because patients often forget how impaired they used to be, and how far they have come due to their hard work and determination. Your therapist will encourage you to identify the components of exposure and response (or ritual) prevention that have helped you the most to get your OCD symptoms under control so that you can use these strategies in the future, without the aid of a therapist or other supporting persons in your life.

Return to Routine Behavior

Your therapist will introduce you to rules of "normal" washing, cleaning, checking, etc. This will enable you to return to what can be considered a routine rather than a ritual.

Relapse Prevention Instruction for Final Session

As mentioned earlier in this book, in the last treatment sessions you and your therapist will be discussing relapse prevention in great detail. The following points will be included:

- As part of reflecting on how far you have come in treatment, your therapist will ask you to re-rate the items on your hierarchy.

- In collaboration with your therapist you will make a list of the strategies that have helped you make these gains. For example: (1) Don't avoid situations just because they trigger your OCD symptoms; (2) Remember what you have learned about exposure: it gets easier with time; and (3) Give up your wish to be 100% certain about things. You can use any or all of these strategies if OCD begins to cause problems for you again in the future.

- Together with your therapist, you will make a specific plan for tackling any issues that may be "left over" after treatment has ended.

- Your therapist will help you make a plan for what to do if relapse occurs.

Scheduling Follow-Up Phone Contacts

Your therapist will schedule four to six follow-up weekly phone calls with you to help ease your transition from the active treatment phase. The function of these phone calls is a brief check-in to troubleshoot any problems that may arise and to help you maintain the gains you made in treatment.

Appendix

Obsessive-Compulsive Disorder: Some Facts

Overview of OCD

It is estimated that approximately 2% to 3% of the population in the United States has obsessive-compulsive disorder (OCD). It has been observed in all age groups, from school-aged children to older adults. OCD typically begins in adolescence but may start in early adulthood or childhood. The onset of OCD is typically gradual, but in some cases it may start suddenly. Symptoms fluctuate in severity from time to time, and this fluctuation may be related to the occurrence of stressful events. Because symptoms usually worsen with age, people may have difficulty remembering when OCD began, but they can sometimes recall when they first noticed that the symptoms were disrupting their lives.

Learning more about your OCD symptoms will help you get the most out of this treatment. OCD is a set of symptoms that, as you may know, include thoughts, feelings, and behaviors that are extremely unpleasant, unproductive, and difficult to get rid of on your own. Usually, these involve thoughts, images, or impulses that come to mind against your will (**obsessions**). These thoughts are accompanied by unwanted feelings of extreme distress or anxiety (or guilt, shame. or disgust) and strong urges to do something to reduce the distress. One way in which people try to reduce their anxiety is by avoiding situations, objects, or thoughts that evoke this anxiety. However, with people who suffer from OCD, avoidance or escape from the things that evoke their anxiety does not work well.

Because, as with all people with OCD, your attempts to avoid the situations or thoughts that cause you the distress do not work well, you developed habits of doing certain actions or thinking special thoughts (**rituals** or **compulsions**) to try to reduce your distress. Unfortunately, performing these rituals also does not work all that well, and the distress decreases for only a short time before coming back again. Often you find yourself doing more and more ritualizing to try to get rid of the distress, but even then the rituals do not reduce the distress permanently, and soon enough you are putting so much time and energy into rituals (that do not work that well anyway) that other areas of your life get seriously disrupted.

The reasons why some people develop obsessions and compulsions while others don't are unknown. Many researchers suggest that people with OCD have abnormal brain chemistry involving *serotonin*, a chemical that is important for brain functioning. Unusual serotonin chemistry has been observed in people with OCD, and medications that relieve OCD symptoms also change serotonin levels. However, it is not known whether serotonin chemistry is truly a key factor in the development of OCD.

There is also evidence that OCD has a hereditary factor and is more prevalent in some families than others. Most likely there is a combination of factors, such as biological/genetic and environmental aspects, that contribute to the development of OCD.

Some experts have suggested that specific "thinking mistakes" occur in OCD. Examples of such thinking mistakes are:

- Unless one avoids the triggers or ritualizes in response to them, the anxiety or distress will last forever or will cause a nervous breakdown

- Thinking about an action is the same as doing it, or wanting to do it.

- If one does not ritualize, the things one is afraid will happen actually do happen.

- If one does not try to prevent harm, it's the same as causing harm or condoning it.

To treat OCD, you will have to learn a new way of addressing your obsessions without resorting to avoidance or rituals. Your therapy is designed to do this, and your therapist knows exercises that will be helpful in achieving this goal. These exercises are called **exposure and response (or ritual) prevention** (EX/RP or ERP), and you will learn more about them in the next session.

Sample Self-Monitoring Form (partially filled out)

Time of Day	Situation/Activity/Thought that evokes the distress and urge to ritualize urge toritual	SUDS (0–100)	Description of ritual	Number of minutes spent on ritual
7 am	Made breakfast	60	Checked stove	10 minutes
8 am	Took out the garbage	70	Hand washing	4 minutes
9 am				
10 am	Bathroom—urination	80	Hand washing	5 minutes
11 am				
Noon	Left house	75	Checked locks	15 minutes

Use the following general rules to guide your monitoring:

- Make sure to record both overt and mental rituals.

- Keep track of the time you spend on your rituals.

- It is best not to save the recording to the end of the day or the beginning of the next day, because you will likely forget details.

- Write a short sentence to describe the trigger for ritualizing.

- Use a descriptive word or two and not a long paragraph for each ritual.

Self-Monitoring Form

Date: _____

Time of Day	Situation/Activity/Thought that evokes the distress and urge to ritualize	SUDS (0–100)	Description of ritual	Number of minutes spent on ritual
6 am				
7 am				
8 am				
9 am				
10 am				
11 am				
Noon				
1 pm				
2 pm				
3 pm				

(Continued)

Self-Monitoring Form (*Continued*)

Time of Day	Situation/Activity/Thought that evokes the distress and urge to ritualize	SUDS (0–100)	Description of ritual	Number of minutes spent on ritual
4 pm				
5 pm				
6 pm				
7 pm				
8 pm				
9 pm				
10 pm				
11 pm				
Midnight				

Appointment Schedule

Wk	Monday	Tuesday	Wednesday	Thursday	Friday
1	—|	—|	—|	—|	—|
2	—|	—|	—|	—|	—|
3	—|	—|	—|	—|	—|
4	—|	—|	—|	—|	—|
5	—|	—|	—|	—|	—|
6	—|	—|	—|	—|	—|
7	—|	—|	—|	—|	—|

- Phone number: _____

- Discuss your assignments with your therapist. Your therapist will want to hear about your progress. You will be able to report on whether you understood the assignment. Indicate how often you were able to do the exposures and for how long. Tell your therapist whether you are experiencing changes in discomfort and urges to perform rituals.

- If any problems arise, write them down before the phone call so that you remember to discuss them during the call.

- If you forgot to do homework, do not avoid telling your therapist. He or she will not be upset with you and will troubleshoot with you about why this happened and help you solve the problem so you can benefit from the practice. By not discussing problems with homework you may affect your own improvement. The therapist can suggest strategies to help with remembering, such as using reminder notes, setting an alarm clock, asking a friend or a family member to remind you, scheduling homework at a regular time each day, etc.

- The therapist will also help you assess the extent to which not doing the homework may be a form of fearful avoidance. If you are avoiding homework because of anxiety, remind yourself that it is expected that one will feel distressed when engaging in exposure. However, it is important to work on the homework despite accompanying anxiety or distress since the long-term payoff is relief from obsessive-compulsive symptoms.

- You might avoid homework exposures because they provoke anxiety about making mistakes. If perfectionism is involved, the therapist will encourage you to do some of the homework imperfectly on purpose, as a way of beginning to practice new habits of doing things "wrong."

- Make sure you know the date and time of the next therapy session.

Cognitive-behavioral therapy (CBT) is a type of treatment that helps individuals cope with and change problematic thoughts, behaviors, and emotions. The treatment you are beginning is a specialized type of CBT for obsessive-compulsive disorder (OCD) called **Exposure and Ritual Prevention (EX/RP)**. Some people refer to the same treatment as Exposure and Response Prevention (ERP). This treatment is designed to help you achieve symptom relief without resorting to engaging in avoidance or rituals. EX/RP consists of four main components: *in vivo* exposure, imaginal exposure, ritual prevention, and processing:

- **In Vivo** *Exposure:* Exposures in "real life" entail deliberately approaching a feared object or situation that evokes anxiety and distress (for example, coming in contact with contaminants and staying in their presence for a period of time; leaving one's possessions in disarray; eating a certain food in spite of fear of throwing up).

- *Imaginal Exposure:* Exposures in imagination entail visualizing oneself in the feared situations, including the consequences of the feared situations (for example, visualizing driving on the road and hitting a pedestrian; losing one's intelligence; contracting a deadly disease).

- *Ritual Prevention:* Entails refraining from ritualistic behavior (for example, leaving the kitchen without checking the appliances; touching dirty laundry without washing one's hands)

- *Processing:* Entails examining the change in your level of distress and in your beliefs after having experiences that disconfirm those erroneous beliefs that are part of your OCD. Exposures will be framed as opportunities to test hypotheses about feared consequences brought on by obsessional distress.

What is Exposure?

Exposure is a procedure in which you purposefully confront objects or situations that you know produce distress and you stay in the presence of those objects or situations long enough for your anxiety to decrease on its own. **In vivo *exposure*** is a type of exposure that involves confronting feared objects and situations in real life. For example, a person who fears contamination by being in a public restroom would purposefully visit a public restroom and stay there for a long enough time to have his or her anxiety begin to decrease. As is often the case, you may believe that your discomfort will escalate or last forever unless you avoid such situations or escape from them when your anxiety or distress starts to rise. You may feel that you couldn't otherwise handle the situation. However, as you will find out, this is not necessarily true. At first you can expect to feel anxiety or discomfort, since these are situations that are designed to activate your fears. However, after repeated exposure practice, such situations will no longer make you feel as uncomfortable as they once did.

Many sufferers have expressed the following bewilderment: If exposure works, why hasn't my distress become less severe through the many encounters with situations that have provoked obsessions and anxiety in the past? The answer is that simply provoking an obsession is not enough. Exposure to the trigger of the obsessional distress requires that it be done for a long enough time to allow the distress to diminish on its own, without removing yourself from the situation or without performing a ritual. In addition, like almost all learning of new skills, the exposure must be done repeatedly to have an optimal effect, thus helping to break the OCD.

Sometimes it is impossible or impractical to actually confront your feared situation and its perceived consequences through *in vivo* exposure. For example, a person may fear that his house will burn down if he does not thoroughly check to ensure that the stove or an iron has been turned off. It would not be a good idea to suggest that the person burn his house down to allow him to confront that kind of fear. Instead, the person can confront the harm resulting from not checking thoroughly by visualizing the house fire in his imagination. In ***imaginal exposure***, you create in your mind a detailed and vivid sequence of images depicting the catastrophic disaster that you believe will occur if you do not avoid or ritualize. As with the *in vivo* exposure, the obsessional distress gradually decreases during imaginal exposure.

Imaginal exposure is also helpful for individuals whose obsessions occur spontaneously and are not triggered by any identifiable situation. For example, a person might have an unwanted and intrusive sexual thought at any time or place. This thought may cause her great distress. In this case, there is no particular situation for the person to confront, and the person can't practice remaining in the exposure situation for a prolonged period of time. With imaginal exposure, the sexual image can be brought up repeatedly, without trying to eliminate it or neutralize it with a ritual.

Imaginal exposure may also be used to make subsequent *in vivo* exposure practices easier for you. If you are extremely distressed about the idea of confronting a situation or object that provokes your distress, you may find it helpful to *imagine* confronting it first. The decrease in your distress during imaginal exposure will carry over to the *in vivo* exposure.

What is Ritual Prevention?

When persons with OCD encounter their feared situations or have obsessional thoughts, they become anxious and feel compelled to perform ritualistic behaviors to reduce the distress. Exposure practices can cause this same distress and the same urge to ritualize. Therefore, in treatment, **ritual prevention** is practiced to break the habit of ritualizing. We know that rituals are difficult to stop because they bring relief from anxiety or discomfort. However, the performance of these rituals is currently greatly interfering with your ability to function in a variety of settings, and is one of the main reasons that you have sought treatment. Ritual prevention requires that you stop ritualizing, even though you are still having urges to do so. Your therapist will teach you how to stop rituals and will introduce you to healthier ways of coping with and managing your distress and discomfort.

What is Processing?

Processing is an important part of EX/RP. It entails a discussion of your experience during or after an exercise using exposure and ritual prevention and what you have learned from that experience. You will realize several facts: (1) Rather than mounting uncontrollably, your anxiety or distress may rise at first but it will eventually begin to fall, even though you are not engaging in avoidance or a ritual. (2) Doing exposures repeatedly results in continued reduction in your distress and helps keep those lower levels anxiety over time. (3) You can indeed manage your distress without having to resort to avoidance or rituals that cost you precious time, a lot of energy, and often money too. (4) You realize that your fears about bad consequences happening if you do not avoid or ritualize is either proven false or shown to have a low probability of actually materializing. (5) Even if your fears of bad consequences cannot be proven wrong, you will learn that you can live with the doubt, the uncertainty and the feeling that you do not have control over events in the future.

An additional optional component of EX/RP treatment is a home visit, which involves the therapist coming to help you with exposures in your home environment. Home visits are conducted on an "as needed" basis and the details decided upon in collaboration between you and your therapist. This is especially helpful if you find it difficult to apply what you have learned during the office visits to your daily activities at home, or if there are subtle avoidance patterns or rituals that would otherwise not be addressed and that are clearly keeping you from benefiting fully from treatment.

Why Should I Do Exposure and Ritual Prevention?

Perhaps you are asking yourself, "Why should I suffer the distress of confronting feared situations on purpose without doing some rituals to get relief?" It is true that after you carry out a ritual, you *temporarily* feel less distress. This temporary relief is what makes you continue to engage in the ritual, which in turn makes your OCD stronger. However, by *not* performing rituals, and learning to tolerate the distress produced by confronting the triggers, you ultimately weaken your OCD, which will improve your quality of life.

How Involved Do I Need to Be in Exposure and Ritual Prevention?

For *in vivo* and imaginal exposure to be helpful, you must become emotionally engaged during the exposure exercises. Specifically, the exposure situation must evoke the same kind of obsessional distress that you experience in your daily life when you encounter these situations. To promote emotional engagement, we will develop exposure exercises that are a good match to the real-life situations that provoke your obsessions and urges to ritualize. For example, if you are distressed by contamination related to cancer and you visit a hospital with no cancer ward, the exercise will not be helpful. This is because the situation does not match your fear, so it will be hard for you to become emotionally engaged.

During the exposure exercises that are a good match to your obsessions, you should pay attention to the distressing aspects of the exposure situation, rather than try to ignore them or distract yourself. This is true for both *in vivo* and imaginal exposure. For example, in the previous example, if you pretend that a cancer ward is really a cardiac unit in order to reduce your distress, the exercise will be less effective. To make the exposure effective, you should think about the potential harm that concerns you. For example, if you are afraid of using public restrooms, a good exposure exercise will be to go to a public restroom. While there, you must think about what concerns you have about the restroom, such as how dirty it might be or what diseases you are afraid of contracting by using it. Similarly, during imaginal exposure, you should include anticipated disasters and focus on imagining them as vividly as you can.

How Can I Get the Most Benefit out of Exposure and Ritual Prevention?

When people hear about exposure treatment, they often do not understand how it works. You might think that if you can just decide to do things that you avoid and give up doing rituals, you really wouldn't need treatment at all. Most people with OCD can temporarily stop their avoidance and rituals, but they find that doing so is very uncomfortable, and after a while they may find themselves wondering why anyone would willingly want to go through it.

Certainly you have had occasions when you accidentally or purposefully confronted feared situations, but your OCD habits persisted. To increase the success of exposure and ritual prevention, you must do well-designed exercises, and do them correctly. In this treatment, exposure exercises will be designed specifically for your OCD symptoms, and your therapist will coach you as you practice them.

What you get out of exposure and ritual prevention depends heavily on what you put into it. It also depends on you and your therapist collaboratively coming up with an exposure plan that fits your particular OCD symptoms. Sometimes exposure exercises may seem counterintuitive or even extreme, but it will be important for you to practice them anyway. A legitimate inquiry is often made by sufferers of OCD whether "normal people" do those extreme things. The answer is that extreme measures are required for extreme disease conditions. So, for example, "normal people" do not get radiation and/or chemotherapy unless they are fighting cancer. You are willingly participating in exposure and ritual prevention in order to best fight your OCD.

Patient Rules for Ritual Prevention

Washing

- During the treatment period, avoid using water on your body for several days. This includes no hand washing, no rinsing, no wet towels, no washcloths.

- The use of creams and other toiletry articles (powder, deodorant, etc.) is permitted unless you find that use of these items reduces your feeling of contamination and/or distress.

- Shave using an electric shaver.

- Water is permitted for drinking and brushing teeth, but take care not to get it on your face and hands.

- Showers are permitted every 3 days, for 10 minutes each—this includes hair washing. Ritualistic or repetitive washing of specific areas of the body (genitals, hair) during showers is prohibited. Showers should be timed by your designated support person, but you need not be observed directly.

- While at home, if you have an urge to wash or clean and you are afraid you cannot resist, talk to your designated support person and ask him/her to remain with you until the urge decreases to a manageable level.

- You should report difficulties with ritual prevention to your therapist.

Checking

- Only "normal" checking is permitted for most items (such as one check of door locks) unless otherwise recommended by your therapist.

- For items ordinarily *not* checked (for example, empty envelopes to be discarded), all checking is prohibited.

- While at home, if you have an urge to check and you are afraid you can't resist, talk to your designated support person and ask him/her to remain with you until the urge decreases to a manageable level.

- You should report difficulties with ritual prevention to your therapist.

Special Instructions:

Exposure Homework Recording Form

1) Situation to practice: _____

_____

Date: _____   Date: _____   Date: _____

	SUDS		SUDS		SUDS
Beginning	____	Beginning	____	Beginning	____
10 minutes	____	10 minutes	____	10 minutes	____
20 minutes	____	20 minutes	____	20 minutes	____
30 minutes	____	30 minutes	____	30 minutes	____
40 minutes	____	40 minutes	____	40 minutes	____
50 minutes	____	50 minutes	____	50 minutes	____
60 minutes	____	60 minutes	____	60 minutes	____

Comments or Difficulties:

2) Situation to practice: _____

_____

Date: _____   Date: _____   Date: _____

	SUDS		SUDS		SUDS
Beginning	____	Beginning	____	Beginning	____
10 minutes	____	10 minutes	____	10 minutes	____
20 minutes	____	20 minutes	____	20 minutes	____
30 minutes	____	30 minutes	____	30 minutes	____
40 minutes	____	40 minutes	____	40 minutes	____
50 minutes	____	50 minutes	____	50 minutes	____
60 minutes	____	60 minutes	____	60 minutes	____

Comments or Difficulties:

Imaginal Exposure Homework Recording Form

1) Exposure exercise that you practiced _____

Date & Time Spent	SUDS			Date & Time Spent	SUDS		
	Pre	Post	Peak		Pre	Post	Peak

Comments or Difficulties:

Imaginal Exposure Homework Recording Form (*Continued*)

2) Exposure exercise that you practiced _____

Date & Time Spent	SUDS			Date & Time Spent	SUDS		
	Pre	Post	Peak		Pre	Post	Peak

Comments or Difficulties:

About the Authors

Edna B. Foa, Ph.D., is a Professor of Clinical Psychology in Psychiatry at the University of Pennsylvania and Director of the Center for the Treatment and Study of Anxiety. She received her Ph.D. in Personality and Clinical Psychology from University of Missouri at Columbia in 1970. Dr. Foa devoted her academic career to study the psychopathology and treatment of anxiety disorders, primarily obsessive-compulsive disorder (OCD) and post-traumatic stress disorder (PTSD). Her research aiming at delineating theoretical frameworks, targeted treatments, and treatment mechanisms of pathological anxiety has been highly influential and she is currently one of the world leading experts in the areas of PTSD and OCD. The treatment program she has developed for PTSD sufferers has received the most evidence for its efficacy and has been disseminated in the US and around the world.

Dr. Foa has published 18 books and over 350 articles and book chapters and has lectured extensively around the world. Her work has been recognized with numerous awards and honors, among them the *Distinguished Scientific Contributions to Clinical Psychology Award* from the American Psychological Association; *Lifetime Achievement Award* presented by the International Society for Traumatic Stress Studies; *Lifetime Achievement Award* presented by the Association for Behavior and Cognitive Therapies; TIME 100 most influential people of the world; 2010 *Lifetime Achievement in the Field of Trauma Psychology Award* from the American Psychological Association; and the Inaugural International Obsessive Compulsive Disorder Foundation Outstanding Career Achievement Award.

Elna Yadin, Ph.D., is a psychologist and director of the OCD clinic at the Center for the Treatment and Study of Anxiety at the University of Pennsylvania. Dr. Yadin received her Ph.D. in Physiological and Experimental Psychology from Bryn Mawr College in 1979 and respecialized in clinical psychology in 1995. Her neuroscience and clinical interests focus on the study and treatment of anxiety disorders, with an emphasis on OCD and PTSD. Her scholarly publications include scientific articles on brain mechanisms of anxiety and relief from fear and on treatment of anxiety disorders in children, adolescents, and adults. Dr. Yadin has been invited to speak nationally and internationally and has taught workshops on the use of evidence-based treatments for anxiety disorders.

Tracey K. Lichner, Ph.D., is a psychologist and director of supervision at the University of Pennsylvania's Center for the Treatment and Study of Anxiety. Dr. Lichner received her Ph.D. in clinical psychology from the Catholic University of America in Washington, D.C., in 2002. Previously at Johns Hopkins University School of Medicine, she participated in research investigating the genetics of OCD. She has conducted comprehensive clinical interviews, nationally and internationally, with hundreds of family members with OCD. At the Center for the Treatment and Study of Anxiety, she has taught in numerous workshops for mental health professionals on the treatment of OCD, PTSD, and grief. Dr. Lichner's professional interests include psychotherapy and the dissemination of evidence-based treatment for OCD, PTSD, and prolonged grief disorder.